EXPLORATIONS

CLIMBING MOUNT EVEREST

BY DALTON RAINS

WWW.APEXEDITIONS.COM

Copyright © 2025 by Apex Editions, Mendota Heights, MN 55120. All rights reserved. No part of this book may be reproduced or utilized in any form or by any means without written permission from the publisher.

Apex is distributed by North Star Editions:
sales@northstareditions.com | 888-417-0195

Produced for Apex by Red Line Editorial.

Photographs ©: Alfred Gregory/Royal Geographical Society/Getty Images, cover, 16–17; iStockphoto, 1, 18–19, 26–27; Shutterstock Images, 4–5, 6, 10–11; D and S Photography Archives/Alamy, 7; Jake Norton/Aurora Photos/Cavan Images/Alamy, 8–9; George Lowe/Royal Geographical Society/Getty Images, 12–13; AP Images, 14–15, 29; Lakpa Sherpa/AFP/Getty Images, 20–21; Gemunu Amarasinghe/AP Images, 22–23; Bettmann/Getty Images, 24–25

Library of Congress Control Number: 2024940536

ISBN
979-8-89250-326-6 (hardcover)
979-8-89250-364-8 (paperback)
979-8-89250-437-9 (ebook pdf)
979-8-89250-402-7 (hosted ebook)

Printed in the United States of America
Mankato, MN
012025

NOTE TO PARENTS AND EDUCATORS
Apex books are designed to build literacy skills in striving readers. Exciting, high-interest content attracts and holds readers' attention. The text is carefully leveled to allow students to achieve success quickly. Additional features, such as bolded glossary words for difficult terms, help build comprehension.

CHAPTER 1
DANGER EVERYWHERE 4

CHAPTER 2
A LONG CLIMB 10

CHAPTER 3
REACHING THE TOP 16

CHAPTER 4
FAMOUS EXPLORERS 22

COMPREHENSION QUESTIONS • 28
GLOSSARY • 30
TO LEARN MORE • 31
ABOUT THE AUTHOR • 31
INDEX • 32

CHAPTER 1

DANGER EVERYWHERE

In the spring of 1953, a team began climbing Mount Everest. The team hoped to reach the mountain's top. Other teams had tried to do this. But none had succeeded.

Mount Everest is in the Himalayas. This mountain range is in Asia.

Many ice chunks fall down the Khumbu Glacier. Some are the size of cars.

The team started on the mountain's south side. Their first challenge was the Khumbu Icefall. It was part of a **glacier**. Its ice could shift and crack. That made climbing very **dangerous**.

TEAMWORK

The **expedition** started with 13 people. But it grew to include more than 400. Several guides showed the way. Porters carried supplies and set up camps.

The 1953 Everest team included climbers, scientists, doctors, and people who took photos and videos.

FAST FACT

Mount Everest is 29,032 feet (8,849 m) tall.

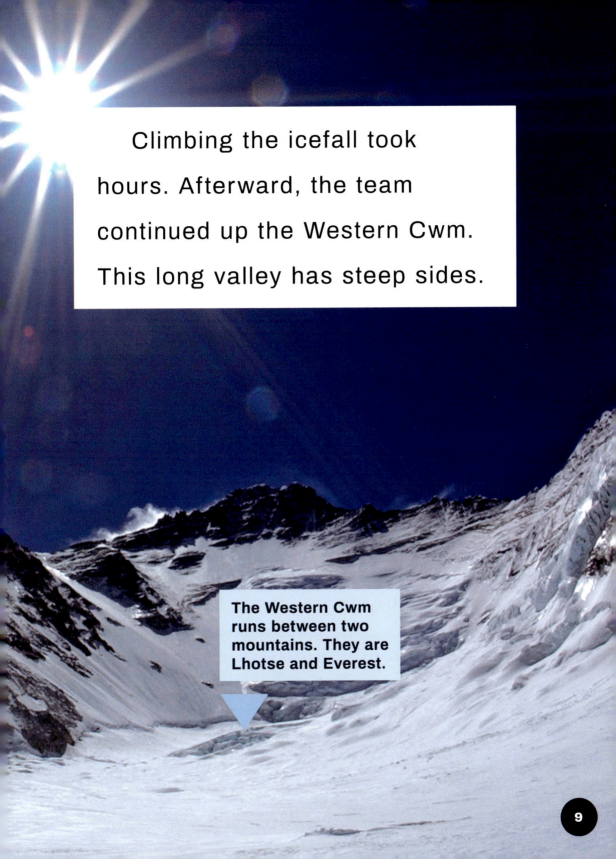

Climbing the icefall took hours. Afterward, the team continued up the Western Cwm. This long valley has steep sides.

The Western Cwm runs between two mountains. They are Lhotse and Everest.

CHAPTER 2

A LONG CLIMB

Climbing the Western Cwm took days. The team set up several camps along the way. One camp was at 24,000 feet (7,300 m). Most climbers waited there.

During long climbs, people stop at camps to take breaks. This helps their bodies adjust to the heights.

Two teams tried to **summit**. Tom Bourdillon and Charles Evans went first. They tried to reach the top on May 26. But they had to turn back.

Thousands of feet up, air becomes hard to breathe. So, climbers use oxygen tanks.

FAST FACT
The first team climbed to about 330 feet (100 m) from Everest's **peak**.

13

So, a second team got ready. Tenzing Norgay and Edmund Hillary climbed to a higher camp on May 28.

On May 28, Hillary (left) and Tenzing climbed to about 28,000 feet (8,500 m).

UNLIKELY DUO

Hillary was from New Zealand. He had started climbing mountains while in high school. Tenzing was from Nepal. He had already climbed partway up Everest several times.

CHAPTER 3

REACHING THE TOP

On May 29, Tenzing and Hillary began climbing at dawn. First, they crossed a narrow ridge. It was about 400 feet (120 m) long. Tall, steep drop-offs plunged down on either side.

A rope linked Hillary (left) and Tenzing together as they climbed.

Near the top of Mount Everest, falls can be deadly. Some cliffs drop down thousands of feet.

Next, they faced a shelf of rock and ice. It was only about 55 feet (17 m) tall. But it was very steep.

FAST FACT
The icy shelf near Everest's peak was later named the Hillary Step.

Today, ropes and ladders help people with the hardest parts of the climb. Early climbers faced more danger.

The men pressed their backs against the rock wall. They used their feet to grip cracks. At 11:30 a.m., they reached the mountain's top.

DEADLY CLIMB

In 1924, two climbers tried to summit Everest. They never came back. No one knew if they had reached the top. Hillary and Tenzing looked for them. But they didn't see any clues.

CHAPTER 4

FAMOUS EXPLORERS

At the top of Mount Everest, Tenzing and Hillary shook hands and hugged. They took pictures. After 15 minutes, they began climbing back down.

Heights above 26,000 feet (8,000 m) are called the "death zone." Humans can't survive there for long.

Tenzing and Hillary met back up with their team. They **descended** together. By June 2, they reached base camp. News of their summit spread quickly.

GIVING BACK

Hillary later joined other expeditions. He also helped build schools and hospitals in Nepal. Tenzing worked to help Nepalese families. He also taught climbing and started a business.

Tenzing and Hillary received awards from the rulers of Britain and Nepal.

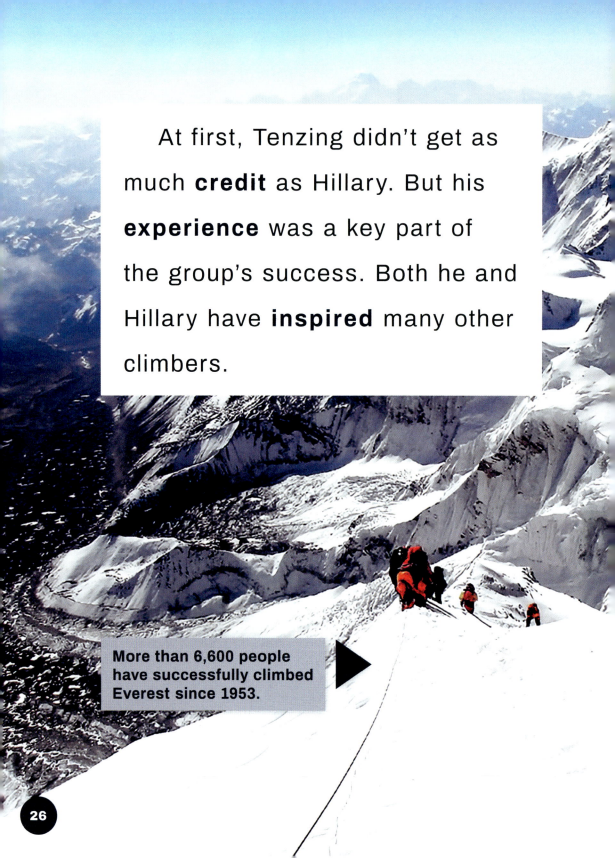

At first, Tenzing didn't get as much **credit** as Hillary. But his **experience** was a key part of the group's success. Both he and Hillary have **inspired** many other climbers.

More than 6,600 people have successfully climbed Everest since 1953.

FAST FACT

Hundreds of people try to summit Mount Everest each year. Not all make it.

COMPREHENSION QUESTIONS

Write your answers on a separate piece of paper.

1. Write a few sentences describing the main ideas of Chapter 3.

2. Would you like to try climbing Mount Everest? Why or why not?

3. On what day did Tenzing Norgay and Edmund Hillary reach the top of Mount Everest?

   A. May 26, 1953
   B. May 29, 1953
   C. June 2, 1953

4. Why did Tenzing and Hillary start climbing at dawn?

   A. so they could have time to climb back down later
   B. so they could reach the peak at night
   C. so they could climb in the dark

5. What does **challenge** mean in this book?

*Their first **challenge** was the Khumbu Icefall. It was part of a glacier. Its ice could shift and crack.*

    A. somewhere that is safe
    B. something that is hard to get past
    C. something that is not real

6. What does **plunged** mean in this book?

*Tall, steep drop-offs **plunged** down on either side.*

    A. split into pieces
    B. jumped into water
    C. dropped down quickly

Answer key on page 32.

GLOSSARY

credit

Praise, fame, or honor for doing an important task.

dangerous

Likely to cause problems or harm.

descended

Went down.

expedition

A group that makes a long trip to reach a goal.

experience

Skills or knowledge gained from doing something before.

glacier

A large, slow-moving body of ice.

inspired

Gave others the idea to do something.

peak

The very top part of a mountain.

summit

To climb to the highest part of a mountain.

BOOKS

Havemeyer, Janie. *Race to Mount Everest*. Mankato, MN: The Child's World, 2020.

London, Martha. *Mount Everest.* Minneapolis: Abdo Publishing, 2021.

Rathburn, Betsy. *Exploring Mount Everest*. Minneapolis: Bellwether Media, 2023.

ONLINE RESOURCES

Visit **www.apexeditions.com** to find links and resources related to this title.

ABOUT THE AUTHOR

Dalton Rains is an author and editor from Saint Paul, Minnesota.

INDEX

B
Bourdillon, Tom, 12

C
camps, 7, 10, 14, 24

D
descending, 24

E
Evans, Charles, 12
expedition, 4, 7, 24

G
glacier, 6
guides, 7

H
Hillary, Edmund, 14–15, 16, 21, 22, 24, 26

K
Khumbu Icefall, 6, 9

N
Nepal, 15, 24
New Zealand, 15

P
porters, 7

S
summit, 12, 21, 24, 27

T
Tenzing Norgay, 14–15, 16, 21, 22, 24, 26

W
Western Cwm, 9, 10

ANSWER KEY:
1. Answers will vary; 2. Answers will vary; 3. B; 4. A; 5. B; 6. C